THE TIMES BETWEEN

JOHNS HOPKINS: POETRY AND FICTION
John T. Irwin, general editor

THE TIMES
BETWEEN

Wyatt Prunty

THE JOHNS HOPKINS UNIVERSITY PRESS
BALTIMORE & LONDON

This book has been brought to publication with the generous assistance of the G. Harry Pouder Fund.

The Johns Hopkins University Press, Baltimore, Maryland 21218
The Johns Hopkins Press Ltd., London

Library of Congress Cataloging in Publication Data
Prunty, Wyatt.
    The times between.
    (Johns Hopkins, poetry and fiction)
    I. Title II. Series.
PS3566.R84T5   811'.54   81-13724
ISBN 0-8018-2403-6   AACR2
ISBN 0-8018-2407-9 (pbk.)

The poems in this volume originally appeared in the following periodicals in slightly different form: *Agenda:* "The Green Lake"; *Canto:* "The Vegetable Garden"; the *Chariton Review:* "A Family Portrait for Our Daughter"; the *Compass:* "Birds That Winter"; *Cumberland Poetry Review:* "You, Mary Dougherty, Living Next Door"; the *Denver Quarterly:* "Repetition"; the *Georgia Review:* "The Kite," "Channel Trout," "Our Tree of Opposites"; the *Literary Review:* "The Flood"; the *Michigan Quarterly Review:* "Summer Rain," "The Widow's Halloween"; *Pequod:* "Seining the Blue"; *St. Andrews Review:* "Gulls at Evening"; *Salmagundi:* "Towards a Relative Ending"; the *Sewanee Review:* "Furlough from the East," "Ballad of the Several Past," "Murals for a Greek Museum," "The Times Between"; *South Carolina Review:* "Winter on the Piedmont"; the *Southern Review:* "Letter," "Death of the Firstborn," "Wallace to Elsie," "The Wake," "Domestic of the Outer Banks," "Another Apollo and Daphne," "The Dancer Who Swims," "Caligula in Blue," "Another Kind of Play," "The Downhill Dream"; the *Virginia Quarterly Review:* "The Effervescent Mrs. G.," "The Insurance Agent," "Forest Fire."

"The Namesake," "An Intermittent Light," and "The Jumper" originally appeared in *Domestic of the Outer Banks* (Inland Boat/Porch Publications, 1980).

"The Letter" and other poems have also appeared in *Poetry Nation Review*.

For Barbara and Heather

Contents

III: THE DOWNHILL DREAM

I

Domestic of the Outer Banks

To become is a movement from the spot, but to become oneself is a movement at the spot.

—*KIERKEGAARD*

The Kite

Away from playground games and fights,
He sings to himself, dancing in the grass,
Steps trailing, a single figure
Intent on the private craft of kites.

It flies because he will not let it go,
Because he wraps the twine around his hand
So tight that blood collects, darkening
Under the wind's insistent tug.

From liquid wrist the string dissolves into its length,
Its curve rising from the ground,
An anchored flight of immobility
And fragile parts strung taut to give them strength.

Vivid for the sky's emptiness,
A bright red patch against the haze and blue,
It soars along a shortened line, but falls
When given run before the wind;

Or like a solitary song's release,
The kite unreels along a spool of thread,
An outward surge over the wind
Flying by the force of being held.

The single master of a vacant lot,
By pulling down it rises up,
This craft of putting fragile things aloft,
Of letting go and holding on at once.

Letter

Today the water whitens over rocks,
Breaking before our eyes into a sound
As constant as the rhythmed strokes
That neighbors make with saws, trimming the limbs brought down
By winter ice;
              the branches crack
As, thrown into the stream, they spin around
Then dart above rocks that, half submerged
Jut moss-green from the mumbled blue, the current's urge.

Three days ago, two miles below the dam,
A boy slipped down in wading clothes,
Trout fishing with his father on the bank;
He surfaced, waved, then slipped again,
Tugging a canvas jacket free to swim.
His father ran along the edge
Then side-stepped to the middle with a limb.
The boy passed by head down.

Grappling lines dragged from either side,
They found him on the second day
Where, slowing, the river widens in a bend:
I stood among the trees and watched,
Immobile in the cooling shade;
He surfaced slowly, face up beneath a bridge
And eyes gazing beyond our grasp
As though he saw at once two sides of blue
And settled for the ground from which he slipped.

2

Cut limbs falling, the crack they make,
Each dropping from its trunk as though for once
The last branch winter made us trim
Was gone for good, more lightly lost for the violence
Of jagged saws, or spring turned whimsical.
The branches lopped, mid-air, mid-stream,
Are casual over the current's drag for them
Till underneath they tumble, breaking stem from stem.

Our stretch of it between the dam and bridge
Runs fast, the water like a path worn new,
Picking its way, wading the land,
As downward deep as upward blue,
At times almost reflecting where a bend,
Slowing, will make the surface calm.
Kept trim, the trees along each bank drink deep
As though one force, and always green, retained their seed.

Death of the Firstborn

With grief each hates as much as loves;
They balance on the moment of this pain,
A passing name that circles from their lives:

Neglecting thought for loss, a broken chain,
Their open-ended process has run out;
The water, spilling, dries into a stain.

There's no one in the corridor to shout,
No catchwords for the separate life each lives;
With mask, he stares her fierceness down to doubt,

Her eyes reflecting in their lowered gaze
On something that was falling from her arms
Till thought, returning, filled a bitter phrase.

Furlough from the East

He waits beyond the light
that squares itself through windows,
fanning across the yard
where, luggage forgotten, he stands in the dark
nervous, jumping as a door slams.
Inside, she moves predictably
from room to room, while he watches
wondering if he will appear
as a bad likeness at the door.

Taut from stalking jungle trails
and waking nights to mortar fire
bracketing his camp, he still patrols
green avenues, aligns objects
down the black plane of an oiled barrel,
his laughter echoing the gun's report.
But here the avenues are so precise
he remembers himself playing
a piano, awkwardly finding his way
through something he knew by heart.

When they meet, she will play, striking each key
more deliberately than he remembers,
more separately as her hands puzzle
to transpose chords like the gaps she feels
between her touch and his reflex.

Wallace to Elsie

Out of the windless house
the still air stands,
nominal and aloof,
and the downturned breathing
catches fire in a thought
wide as the green yard
growing between green hedges.

Looking back, the windows
square in their curtains
like so many resolutions,
half public, half private,
or like a series of gestures
made self-consciously.

Eaves shadow walls against all kinds
of change, the season, the weather,
but not this stillness which waits
in its silence much as the seeds
you bought us months ago that also wait
in their dark, dry boxes.
My downturned breathing
interrupts itself uneasily.

Inside, a radio plays,
the washer hums virtuously,
and the musical plumbing chimes
between walls as the plumb house stands
on a hill that overlooks still air;
as one thought, clear and aloof.

High in a window in the windless house
your profile catches my glance as I
transplant small dogwoods, their slim trunks
already bent.
                    The green yard greens
between stiff hedges, and dogwoods bloom
in shade where nothing else will grow.
Your profile holds. I work toward where you watch.

Raking the Drive

The state hospital has sent
our neighbor home again.
He leans over
a borrowed rake
and tells his son
the origin of gray rocks
now gathered in
a muddy jar,
or tells me what
investments he would make,
the market being
what it is. He plans
for an office nearer
home, to walk
to work fair day
and foul, leaving the car
or selling the car,
but walking to work and home.

The blue jays
are at war again;
the next-door cat
is on parade. It stalks
beneath the boxwood hedge,
catching chameleons
then letting them go,
re-attacks.
Our neighbor plans to trim
the hedge another way,
and feed the cat
and rake the rocks,
smoothing the hump
that ruins his drive
while he is walking home
with empty hands
or waking to
tranquillity,
tying his shoes
as separately as
possible.

A Family Portrait
for Our Daughter

All night the nurses let me listen,
your heart like hobnail boots down corridors.
The pain is rhythmical, and we talk between
your urgencies, watching the clock
for more of you, pressed and pressing.
Positions much like tools with no handles,
your mother shifts from chair to bed to chair,
breathing with forced-march regularity.
Later, diminuendo on a side porch
where instruments are fading out of tune,
the funny way the mind deflects from pain.
Then there you are, a late result
of leisurely lust and evolution,
your mother smiling over you
out of the womb and endlessly crying;
though innocent, already apprehensive.

Genetically, I'd mix you like Matisse
in a garden's green concert of senses,
fluidity of feeling marveling where
the eye's despotic glance focuses then blurs.
Nearsighted, you cause us to draw close;
we wonder what you see of us,
a Dutch guild portrait with possessive eyes
blinking each time the flash goes off?
Such pictures lie in spite of us.
Outside all photographs, this fact,
you cry full of a shower's present tense.

You, Mary Dougherty, Living Next Door

Almost too loud, you called us toward your terrace,
always the laughter and large flowers blooming,
over watered, you always over watered;
your ferns eclipsed the soil with their gills.
My wife and I, our baby and you—
first on your terrace, then in your room,
and then the old downtown hospital,
the humid air too close to catch a breath.
Your daybed-reasoning held drift
through redolent mums, arranged but out of reach,
stationed atop your vanity
like one last Victorian appointment.

Veneer, the Brownian dust on dark veneer,
and your husband's luggage kept for just now,
the last train gathering, conductor poised—
much as a cold front clears the sky
you pushed beyond your humid room;
nurse and doctor, and their white gestures
reasoning wilderness, and you outside
as unobtrusively as only
the most deft and polite of large women
whose plants eclipse their origins.

The Namesake

A sister on the way, I was farmed
Out to my grandmother in Tennessee—
Picked Presbyterian her entire life
And reading Tennyson when I arrived
To spend all summer on her "home farm."
Once she taught Elocution to children
Who could not spell and whose "rise in life
Always stalled at local heights." They were determined.
And so was she, even reading "Tennusin"
With clipped enunciation.
                  But the world
I heard was never clipped; it ran beyond
The tree lines whose shadows framed the farm
Into a lush mid-air where all
Was waiting and nothing arrived.
Even the clock seemed stalled that summer,
As though we'd never get past 1954.

This year we skip the interstate,
Making our way rectilinearly
Back to the farm whose predestined crops
Grow like conservative bankers.
Another sister's on the way.
Her great-grandmother rises and stalls,
Greeting us through a screen; someone clips
The hedge beneath her window.
Beginning now, again life starts,
Swelling before a name, the seed so placed
That casually one bird alights,
Grasping the branch so many miss;
Much as an intervale crowds green each spring,
The snow's white riot flowered on the bough.
The water, having swollen into flood,
Resumes arterial calm, reflecting.

The Wake

In Newbern Tennessee he lies awake
Listening to the rocker's creaking rungs;
Downstairs the old man nodding in the dark,
His head bobbing eccentric pendulums,
Disturbs the quiet of one sleep.
The winter night is clear and cold,
Carrying noises farther than ever,
Beyond the house, the northwest field,
The lane that borders, rutted and washed.

Hardwoods, audible in a sharpened wind,
Blend with long whistles from the freight
Whose engines rumble through the center of town
And fade again with echoes like a chill.
Downstairs the old man is rocking in dark
Or should be, as the chair is creaking still;
The house is creaking in the winter wind,
Filled like a family's hard-breathing sleep
That, cooling, moves from room to room.

The Effervescent Mrs. G.

Retainer of the bridge club win and loss.
Perhaps the numbing fall is always painless
like a good block or uppercut
that knocked you out.

Regarding the scar of a Christmas sunset,
she said there was no fear of time
but there was always curiosity
for the hours spent over coffee or sherry.

When the obituary became
a catalogue of world events,
she would address a grandson with the name
of his dead uncle, using a timeless logic.

She walked with the poise of a polite drunk
the captain of a reeling deck;
swaying in the hall mirror, she once remarked
that every house should have a picture window.

Lately, surveying the perimeters
of an upstairs bedroom,
she addressed a ten-watt bed lamp
and wept for Jesus like a toy drum.

Her timeless dress, her quick smile
have become frozen in the blue light
of a diamond, a mirror,
a window's face framing the mad moon.

Bright curtains caught in an opened sash,
a curious love, curiosity kept her long
living on coffee and sherry. But a cold
scratched, filling one lung, then another.

Summer Rain

The children play Simon says
under oak trees. They laugh
while the garden hose
cuts them with a peppered arc.

The converse of your smiling mouth,
of cocktails on the lawn
and a once quipped line,
"fabric woven by the moth,"
distracts me for a moment:
The air is fragrant,
and the game's riot eases where twilight
resolves into the blue vapor
of the streetlight by our house.
It will be supper and bed soon,
the brief objection, the burst of tears
with toys left among trees,
all kissed with clean linen and prayers.
Perhaps they find what they have seen,
a discovery dreamed prior to waking.

On the porch the air cools then rushes
as we watch lightning peel the bark
from an oak standing above the sprinkler
which now waves its monotonous arc
invisibly in the rain. Your mouth
has the odor of that rain, which
patterns near the light then skews with gusts.

Canaries

For their safety, we keep them caged
and at home, available all times,
as peering as peered at. In the park
there are eagles and hawks tethered to stumps
and doves in a glass cage never quite clean.
We hold our daughter's hands and walk;
a man describes the factual floor
of zoo survival, municipal ark
but amid what rainbowed flood?
Imagine their power in flight.

Heads tilted and preened
in the parrot's mirror,
we keep pets within and without,
peered at and peering, ourselves
and our mascot daughter holding hands,
urging the birds from farthest corners
yet treating the cut-end branch
of instinct as a perch.

Domestic of the Outer Banks

For days the house is dark and slightly cold;
the wind is locked in curtains, in cupboards,
is damply waiting on the cellar stairs
while fever burns beneath a single sheet.

She skims the room with shallow lungs for breath;
her eyelids close by white and blue degrees
to patterns thrown upon a screen like paint,
like aqua over sand in rhythmed sleep.

Here is the final illness of her age,
the pulse and watch unwinding into air
that waits between the walls and floors for fire,
for heat to draw the flesh to bony form.

Sick for an animate face
and single name to call this house,
taut in the linen of a worn estate
with failing mind to grace the end, she waits

condemned to province and imagined health:
Diluting measures of the medicine,
the lips drawn tight to smile,
she listens for familiar names and dates,

for seagulls calling past the window sill
to hover and to plunge.
                              They plunge again
and she is thirty; the black-tipped birds
are things that slice from air into the sea,

are paring knives set to their memory.
The wings divide upon her severed air
like hydras in a sensual wave
that will not unfold or give release.

Ballad of the Several Past

Here is a man, his ticket stamped.
Alone in line and looking down,
this time he boards an all-night train,
finding a seat and stretching out;
uninterrupted movement helps him sleep,
he thinks, then leans his head against the glass:

With gentle roll and rhythmic tick
the rails suggest an open-ended trip
through moonlit fields of grain,
a metronomic land where harvest yields
old quantities required or stored
for travelers regaining rest.

A jolt. His head snaps back; he starts awake
then slips again:
                          Revolving scenes,
selecting one,
                    a room where dinner cools,
his parents laughing until their eyes tear,
napkins used as handkerchiefs,
a family joke they value for the telling.

That room again, the sun igniting dust
on dark veneer and no one there.
                                            Outside,
houses recede across successive fields
as trains unwind along rails.
The miles consume wide fields,
transporting harvest dry as death.

The Insurance Agent

He gathers at the base to take a breath,
to shuffle up the attic steps
and fumble with a light switch in the dark.
The bare bulb glares in pendulums of light,
shadowing scattered toys and chairs,
curled photographs and wedding clothes.

Agreement is a document unsigned,
a rotting beam in the angular wall;
equity, a broken rocking horse,
the rummaging order of attic shelves;
and solvency, discarded clothes
hung threadbare in permanent sway.

He throws the attic window wide
and scans Orion's ancient hunt
repeating itself, a hollow sapphire
coldly focused on his focusing eyes.

Winter on the Piedmont

Tonight we watch the process of our talk
in sliding doors so black they mirror us;
two worlds recording gestures that we see
reflected as from underneath a pool.

Outside, the wind is sawing through pines,
exhausting the single running mind
that strains to measure everything it hears,
cold and sharp under winter stars.

It saws all night, and I sleep in a draft
dreaming of evergreens on the piedmont,
their boughs reflected in a stream
that flows from caves but, going, remains

with fish suspended like Chagall's,
like kites strung flying from the touch.
The fixtures of a windy, falling dream
with heads reflecting in a broken shaft

that empties out of darkness,
I dream the blind eyes of white fish are stars
sketched across a fragile screen
framing memory into light.

Revising
Boundaries

Seining the Blue

A reservoir we cannot see across.
We walk its shallow parts counting the bream
that dart from sight before our march,
admiring the bass that will not leave its nest,
and we seine for only the proper size.
The small slip through; some others, thrown back in,
wriggle into the grass and hide,
but the rest are raised fighting against all nets.

A hook-and-line in singular play
requires more craft than this; the patient lead
and setting barb seem oddly intimate,
as if the line, let out, conjoined two elements:
a quiet man fixing his sight
over a surfaced calm and something else
below that calm violently lost,
                              the line
rigid, a bass down deep refusing force.

Each spring the reservoir backs up and clouds
then fosters fish and clears predictably.
Because each catch proves more
than we can surface,
we watch what moves beyond our net
where whitecaps blue from overhead
then darken in the water's depth;
transparencies of eye and lake.

Channel Trout

He wades waist high to fish for channel trout,
the wind low-leaning and alive,
curling and spuming the whitecaps to spray—
he casts his line, weighted yet arced by the wind.

Bracing the waves, he reels the line,
lead sinker, hook and bait
over a silt-clouded and shifting floor
to take the strike;
                    the sudden drag, arms taut,

the clicking reel retrieves to its spool
a low-diving and startled thing,
gathers, gears ticking, into the net
a finning trout that gulps the air and drowns. . . .

Its lidless eyes grow cloudy in the sun,
cloudy with scaling and with fire;
the fisher looks through level wine in a tilted glass
for shadows on a long and silent line.

Repetition

The hardening innocence
of a boy's eyes locked on his mother
dying, all questions set aside,
his father bends beyond their gaze
into the fold of similar hands
repeatedly clasping the same defeat.
No memory serves this fact.

The several patterns mourners take,
as though the ritual put
their blackening thoughts from them;
all, public in the ignorant eye
and anxious to the final touch,
detailed habits keeping questions
where memory folds with calloused hands.

Mother gone, the father's hand curves
but to what purpose over
such towhead wondering, and will.
Resentful love perhaps but towering
cold generation to the repeated act
of self out of self in a breath
that drawing in must also let out.

Turning, much like the album sift
of parents and their dead parents,
the ironical head tilts,
genetic beyond place; the hand print holds
just where each calloused touch lets go.

The Flood

Retrace the course. Running upstream,
we sail full speed three days
until the river shallows near its source
then anchor to revise our charts; what seemed
navigable is not, and where there were channels
silt is settling from the flood.

Marking the depth, we drift downstream
checking the inlets of tributaries
and noting the current's gathering speed,
remeasuring what only measured seems
to stay in place. Reporting, we say:

The source is shallow and clear;
running downstream, the body grows,
bearing little resemblance to itself.
It fills with mud, with wood and trash
as branch after feeding branch empties for the mouth.

A Long Day's Dying

Yours is the deep cruise, the downed sub
not heard from again, diving too late,
past help, sailing beneath our common dream
of ports made safe from storms at sea.
With failing valves, the gauges wait,
dropping; the hull has gently settled on sand.

In factories progressive-dies are stamping
figures out, rolling the parts down belts
where each joins each, producing one from two.
They make the means by which you pushed the bolt . . .
slow motion, narrowing view
until you were still, beyond insane:

Now only rumors fill your mental gap,
disturbing its gulf when waked or scared
by the verbal collage of a name.
You have put your hand through the fist you made,
fished in the air with perfect nets and seined
from one the two you argued for, have strained
and found that, severed, you were only parts.

The Vegetable Garden

Needled by death for change, for simple change,
We turn the soil,
                    another season's crop
Growing from seed, from rain and last year's rot
Into a fruit we never arrange:

The lettuce outgrows our appetite,
While fences smother with towering beans
And tomatoes swell from the dark of their roots;
All tactile reaching for decay turns green

And hangs in the spray of a garden hose.
Dripping with light, the leaves must bow,
Darkening under shadows we cast
Walking among each picked, each weeded row.

Seasons are canned into lines along shelves,
Are named and dated while vinegar boils,
Filling the house with an acrid smell,
And vines are turned beneath themselves:

Our garden is a form that answers cost,
And, growing out of hand with constant care,
Distinctions bloom, ripen, rot and bear
Into the gathering grasp of something lost.

The Breaking Child

In my house the walls are not true;
Floors fit an oblique resolution
No carpenter's square can reconcile.
At night the wind whistles a crazy air,
And someone plays the sticks across the roof.
Ragtime gusting, the ridgepole dials
Under an incomplete geometry;
Shingle to shingle, the rhythm hoofs
A dance that is measured by miles.

My parents' furniture bulks where movers
Have left it. Unable to sleep, I trace
My hand on wood, deep-veined with burnishing.
Outside, the sky blows cold and clear;
Stars slue about the oblique foundation,
And the wind lobs limbs, waving,
Like upraised hands waving above a drop
Too deep to feel, yet welcoming connection.
Somewhere below a voice begins to sing:

And the house contains, all musicale,
The celestial spheres rolling from room
To room, unseasoned floor,
Defiant carpenter.
                    Whose hand-me-down is this?
Blue entering black, the sky is veined with limbs.
You, my parents, sing where wind has closed the door;
You grieve the tree line's seeded cut,
Years of fencing, the yard so hemmed
You stand apart looking beyond, living before.

Gulls at Evening

Now set against
the context of the sky,
excited birds in
thin outline
are rising
on their quick
down-thrusting wings,
circling over
cluttered shores and the cries
of young waiting below.
Intuitive,
their flights are
flights of sudden starts,
hollow bones
and beating wings,
scanning eyes scavenging
for the dried outlay of waves.
Each call dissolves
with calls,
with distance dies,
their narrow wings
fading over the sand
then rounding back,
moving against the wind
more slowly now
as they descend,
answering cries.

An Intermittent Light

Evening paper under one arm,
I whistle my way briskly home.
The sun enlarges red till twice
Its size, the sky a dark relief
Of clouds knotting, then stretching from sight.
White pines still catch the sun's half disk
And burn with a green clairvoyance,
More fiercely for the shade they give.

Tonight the sky is translucent,
And houses wedge beneath as if
Diminished light intensified
Their interiors to certain space.

Rounding the corner to our street,
I wonder at our house, its small contrast.
Inside, you're sitting underneath a lamp;
The light is circular, and I am late
To a room that already arranges
Where we will sit and what we will say.

Think of the shadows underneath each tree
Dissolving, how the ambling mind
Must look for ways to cut beyond
Where, finding it circles, it fades;
Much as outside the window where we sleep
There are distances we never talk about,
Something in the way trees take the light
But, waking, we surface to their shade.

The Green Lake

The stillness sinks as we turn back
Into the rising sleep of settled lakes,
Green water deep with grass, reflected trees
Still young along the banks that hold us here.

I dream we fly beyond the careful hedge
Of properties we cannot count or keep,
Extended fields that tree lines cut with shade,
A landscape rolling under the sun
Rhythmically as the rise and fall
Of water on soft banks that slide from view.

All summer sleeps each afternoon with us.
The lake grows still, its surface warm,
Inviting dives that step from sleep to air,
That break the calm by knifing down
To a quieter, colder green.

Reruns

This fall the trees fire red and gold;
The sun hangs, adamant in the cold
As dusk deepens the room where we sit.
We watch the news and wince at it,
The screen's squared field delineating fear,
Our daughter playing underneath;
The film-clipped war's hieratic grief
Serialized, year after slow-bleeding year.

Cartoons depict the hero's saving grace:
Tight jawed, he makes the rules, can win the chase
Or tear his adversary limb from limb. Nerves twitch,
Joshua turned *Übermensch;*
Much as the athlete's choice, reflex
And gesture seen as one response,
Dated at once, repeated at once.
Each generation feels its muscles flex.

Suppose that standing armies run in place:
The close-up sergeant's sweating face
Grows redder with each cadence that he counts;
His gladiator jowls have jounced
All afternoon, and still the army stands.
The order to "move out" too quick for grief,
The youthful minds that march would not believe
What the sergeant understands.

Murals for a Greek Museum

Not modern lovers enfolding themselves,
Lying beneath the blankets where they reach
For images of those they do not hold
Till sleep engulfs them, binding up the breach

But old-fashioned lovers, elegant with ease,
Who, knowing there is craftsmanship, have learned
Collected smiles and who, fixing their eyes,
Have fostered gods while nature turned.

These, imagined and painted on a wall,
Return the looks of passers-by
Gazing widely along the hall
For exchange in the pigment of an eye;

Staring out of the sky's blue mouth,
As silently as clouds collide they unite
In the draft of a wind's apparent path
And turn their gathered shapes into their sight.

Another Apollo and Daphne

—for Robert Graves

Naming her, he calls into a word
His love which gathers and returns the name,
For echoed with distance, she remains
Between his speaking and her wood.

The tree line where his call repeats is evergreen
And entered proves his reason lost;
Exploring in the absence that she lives,
He cannot see beyond the branches' screen:

The calloused bark and shining leaves
Will not relent, so he must bid his love
Become the fruit of laurel and evergreen,
His god's intent praising her silent grove.

The Dancer Who Swims

*It is supposed to be the most difficult task for a dancer to
leap into a definite posture in such a way that there is not
a second when he is grasping after that posture.*—Kierkegaard

Something like Brahms, lineal and alone,
Always an uncertain act, performed in parts:
You turn; the music starts,
Its rhythm carried into lines
Whose antic and bright argument
Become a myth you map, dancing where we forget.
The movement drugs; its meaning slips
Each time you step beyond the spotlight's lap.
Suggestive angles opening,
Half circles close. And yet when done
Recalled as lineal, recalled alone;
Singular steps, delimiting lines.

The movement of your force, just as precision ends.
Wet tendons twist beneath each turn;
We blink our eyes, St. Vitas bends
As, coiling upward, muscles loosen over bones.
After a time, the lights go out;
The night help comes to sweep away what's left.

Think of a silted lake where the lone diver swims.
He does not see a lake, but swims alone
Circled by a darkness that opens
And closes just as he moves. Perspective—
A disk, the spotlight's lap.
Turning, he views where he has kicked silt up
And cannot see just where he was,
But if he swims ahead then circles back,
He recovers that sedimented past,
Almost the same, a landscape kicked and clouded
Yet reminiscent, edging between
That thing expected and what was found:
Much like the green in a tree
But only that green after the last ring
And before the nudging bark.

Again. The surface of that silted lake
Reflects angling branches overhead,
Bent yet widening with growth.
This time, a boy swims, his curling arms
Half circles wheeling into view,
Then out of view; the lake, its runnels
Branching underneath, reflects where he tries
Both surface and the deeper cool beneath
As if his were the gestures from a wider dance.
Wavering arms, uncertain sequences,
A figure thrusting into air
Who momently holds himself aloft.

III

The Downhill Dream

Forest Fire

Set loose on the hills to tramp all night,
To crawl beneath the season's leaves
Or tower into trees with searing light
And breathe upon a bright framework of limbs,

The fire proceeds before the wind,
A liquid light of tongue curled upon tongue
And waves of heat that hypnotize the eye,
That beckon one to walk within.

The blaze exhales and we retreat foot after foot
Like soldiers from an ancient war
With meaningless shields tempered to reason,
Reflecting the night's black wick and flame:

The leaves of every branch struck like a match,
The toppled oak consuming from the ground;
All night the hills are loud with falling trees,
Are bright with foliage eating from its branch.

The Jumper

As the sportscaster raising his voice
and hurrying words, I praise your skill,
your sudden thrust and cleared fall
made as you threw yourself
out of bounds, beyond our rules
more absolute than we like to think.

Returning from a fishing trip, I passed
the town's high water tower
where you stood looking up till you leaped.
That night, I dreamed my son
took the same step into a clear pool
where he surfaced laughing and bobbed like a cork
waiting for the hooked drag and undertow
that his line, let out, must follow.

Your rejection questioned us all.
The dumb police stared at you lumped
on the close-cut grass,
and firemen leaned against their trucks
looking away as if to the next call
where things were different,
where someone cried for help
and they could answer.
Only the animate newsman wanted to talk,
but he couldn't imagine,
as a real sportscaster would,
how your last move must have been made
before you had the time to think,
much as the athlete's answer is reflex.

The Widow's Halloween

The pumpkin's hollow head returns her gaze;
His yellow eyes are dancing in the flame,
And she, she has him on her window sill
Within a draft that flickers on his brain.

His jagged smile and diamond eyes
Are mirrored in the darkened panes,
Set to be seen, not see, to blaze before the wind
Or wither on the wick and snap out cold.

Grinning backwards into the room,
On either side and looking in,
His gaze, she feels, was sharply cut
To burn beneath her dresses' hems

Or follow her when reaching for the broom.
She wears the latest fashions as her age
But feels the flicker of his gaze
And will not pass near him.

The Times Between

—for Florence, Minnie, and Mary

The severe dancer poised before her mirror
Waiting for the music to begin;
Or academic nude, arms parabolic
Above the students of one pose:
For you that all was years ago,
Ward-Belmont, what little Nashville offered;
Half-gentlemen from Vanderbilt,
Starched collars bent to every healthy bustle.

Now it's the times between you must control.
Late afternoon when vacancy
Invades the room, even the sun porch
Lightens half-heartedly. It's like a lull
In conversation that's never taken up
But leaves each feeling vaguely responsible,
The retarded gust of a ceiling fan,
Too slow to cool, but always turning.

You, who taught us guilt and humor,
Your stories bringing laughter till we wept,
Would take us swimming, though afraid to swim;
Head heavier than feet, you said,
Don't go too far; and thus we always did.
Tonight, you swim beyond our call, and we
Must stand waiting. Regard us now,
Waving you towards the amplifying shore.

Caligula in Blue

What I have to tell you is the rain.
And that I am poor without you.
Here, the weather's all we reason by:
the sky blues overhead then clouds collect,
our summer storms repeating themselves
redundantly against the ground.
We look for rainbows out of here
in snapshots where the register is wrong;
I touch your picture by my bed
then recollect myself and wait, listening.
The rain outside has drummed retreat.

Rain and the redundant ground,
erosion is the only way we leave.
I hear hot water through the pipes
when I bathe, in my tropical ease;
the harbor's mouth is porcelain,
the drain's whirlpool, infinity.
Diminished apertures, I see myself,
a cavern finding water through a fault.

My roommate's like retarded light,
the landscape on a sill where dreams assert
an endless now. We sit in bed and watch
the Late Late Show, finding
the viewer's mind must frame and pan
until the weather lets him sleep:
The rain spatters my notebook near a sash;
the manic wind is up, tearing leaves all night,
and I dream those leaves bleed and talk of you.

Awake at 6 A.M., the sky grays;
blank aperture, then blank response,
which makes me think the mind refracts itself
discursively, in a round country
where kind finds kind, and locks its gaze:
you've written me our daughter has my eyes,
my roommate has them too; he lounges
in a parrot shirt and reads my chart
critically. Asked his name, he colors
like a circus tent, then stammers
he has forgotten, but will remember.
When he can sleep, he dreams a rainbow;
like mine, his spectrum is a glance turned blue.

My dear, the allegory in
my parrot talk has died here
where doctors dart like sparrows, speaking
prismatically, their conversations
ranging over the months I can't recall
while, eraser clean, I kept my pencil sharp.
Why must the cogito and cockatoo
always be caged together?
If mortality's the odd game love repays,
why does the parrot shirt laugh blue when I weep fire?

The Family Act

The big top billowing
over lines and poles,
its brightly colored
sections clash
as husband and wife
climb their ladder
and, introduced,
dive calmly into space.

Swinging above
the sawdust ground,
one meets the other,
catching her fall with
hand on wrist then,
turning around,
releases her
to twirl away.

The curve of the caught
fall is their serious play;
over a darkened ring,
the nets let down,
they live by taking
leave of those
who move them most
to stay.

Another Kind of Play

When it continues, he watches her door,
Imagining her arrested face
As she rearranges tables and chairs
Then moves about, sweeping her intricate floor.
She will not see the doctor,
Ignores him when he mentions it; instead,
When it starts, much as a child finds
A task to make a game, she sweeps the floor.
A mousetrap taut and out of the way,
Set where the house turns recessively small,
Snaps each night without waking them.
He sets it new each day.

Late afternoon she likes the way
The tanagers dart for suet and seed,
And when the field mice run under the feeder
She will not let him scare them away.
On the terrace at night the air is close
Over their conversation;
Azaleas needing water, he moves the hose
And hears the change tightening in her voice
As she corners herself, urging a wall.
It happens that fast, articulate
Their most inarticulate passion,
A swinging door that leaves him small.

The Downhill Dream

Along a slope the river quickens pace.
Erupting over rocks, it proves its force
Then slows and curls reflectively, a race
That runs the angular course
Of an aging man caught in a downhill dream:

"These are the shortened days before the freeze,"
He thinks, turning, walking above the stream;
"The unmarked days beyond each branch's leaves
That concentrate the beauty of a passing thing,
A passing thought rippled in this cold intent.
What will the water, freezing, change?
What answers can an April sun extend
To one who, walking months before,
Imagines all that greens and flows again?"

Again he turns and, turning, feels that change.

Cold on the cloudless sky the birds retreat,
All altitude and patterned flight;
This time the course runs south, not down,
And shallow ponds reflect their migrant paths,
Thin flights informed before the cold
Of lengthened nights, bright wing-eliding days—
All, questions that their cries create.

The slope of the downhill dream releases
Bird and man to migrant thoughts of warmer
Days and longer light, to russet grass,
Forgiving fields with wide intent,
A landscape grown ecstatically still,
Forever in the teasing mind:

Old areas, new gates across
Recurrent paths, the wearing ways
Of animals, of men returning home;
This downward tumbling claptrap reach
And rearranging hope for permanent May.

Birds That Winter

Rising over the wind then circling
For space to light, they do not go;
Silent and small, aloft in the changing air
They flutter then glide as if they know,
Their wings applauding the dusk, the time of year
That deepens among darkening trees.

At night, white pines loud in the quickening air
Roll under stars like stationing lights,
And the cut red clay beneath their trunks
Hardens with frost, with ruts like ragged stairs
To trip one gazing at local heights
Where birds huddle and fold to sleep.

Stiff in the cold, each limb points out, away
Where migrants to a greater height will fly,
The sky almost a black veneer
Covering this wood that grows and stays
Beyond a time of year, that does not die
While the small and cold are wintered here.

The Woodcutter

If then the mind wishes to apprehend itself as creator, it must recognize in its act of creation an act of annihilation. —Poulet

I still hear him in the spring when, windows up,
the wind rifts leaves and I look out
expecting to catch his bent frame
passing among trees he will cut.
Or I hear him late at night
when, suddenly awake, I listen:
He is in the window fan's white noise,
working alone, seven days a week,
thinning the woodlot by our house.

Well into his seventies,
every afternoon I heard his
aphoristic swearing, which echoed past
the woods' provisional edge.
Scruboak and locust, or maple when warm
catching the saw's teeth at every thrust,
each time the woods came crowding in
Jack said he made a path, cutting
randomly until he found a clearing
worth his pause.
                        His moving through the trees
became their green procession past my gaze
until the labyrinth of paths he cut
puzzled out of sight into themselves.

Some nights he stopped to tell me how
that day a hollow's deep proximity
of vines thickening over rotting stumps
made him think that he was watched:
Neck stiff in a chill that feathered leaves,
he felt the hidden eyes and pictured what they saw . . .

a tree's notched trunk vibrating just before
it kicks back out above the limbs'
appointed crash and settling dust.

I saw a man who walked head bent as if
some pride had gotten upside down in him,
an experimental god
whose domain was another's wood,
and yet whose sweat condensed with purpose,
like resignation, but without reserve,
a sort of negative that gathered strength
with every tree cut down. Another Adam
in a tall garden, he named the views
each trunk allowed and memorized
the paths that made the distances
in which to think each fall toward spring.

Once he said he was a child asleep
in its own life, like fall when the year's growth
stalls into waiting. Always for him
the future tumbled in a quiet breeze,
much like a stand of meadow grass
that, deep with itself, changes color
green into green as the wind combs.
Trees were spontaneous under his ax,
curt properties just where the sunlight cut
half days, centripetal calms;
light slanting till October's flaring pause
and vivid equilibrium
made final push into a cold
darkening time, a time past cutting wood.

Jack died much as he worked;
not in the quiet terminus we thought
but like an unveiled bust whose look is wrong,
the rigid mouth and startled eyes,
an intrinsic self beyond self sympathy.
What I heard then, I always hear
when half asleep or startled awake
by the fan's white noise:

Leaves shed like voices crying in
a wind that hollows huge rooms
opening each minute into miles.

Rising, what I see outside are
the innumerable trees, both planned
and random, and walks cut years ago
still visible to anyone who follows;
intensifying green, earth's radical,
the cut-down tree creates a path,
falls to a means for seeing, a way
for walking into woods, and walking out.

Marriage in Woods

At dark cicadas start like rain,
A casual rain heard daily until
Not heard at all. Nothing will grow from it,
No ground erode or new stream train
Into arteries. No seed will set.
Genetic futures locked like bloodstone,
Behind the sound of rain the first water clock
Has taken measure. Someone has made a bet.

The dancer learns to lean through her stillness,
Filling space for as long as we watch.
Her dance turns play, takes place in thought,
Someone thinking another stillness
That surrounds her periodic steps
Much as cicadas fill the dark
That circles the polarity of our light
So completely we think the sound has stopped.

The old, inadequate area
Empties again, the hurried purchase
And short way home, a calendar we keep
Years out of date, or a barrier
We reach for like an empty cup,
Listening for the rain to start.
We know it will start, the cicadas quiet now
As an audience that feels all time has stopped.

We are leaning through our stillness,
Two trees about to fall, the opened land
And wind gathering,
                    two dancers, eyes
Lost in a moment's forgetfulness
Of the insect world that eats and dies,
And does not matter. No clock can count
The doubleness we buy. We feel our time take
Place in thought and, leaning, learn to multiply.

The Nineteenth Hole

—for Matt,
dead somewhere in Saigon

Now all the balls your daddy hit
have been shagged. The nineteenth hole is
full,
    and honor's safe on
the next golf cart teetering
through the greening rough.
The bunker yawns unforgivably
as, putters out, a foursome ambles
between dink shots on close-cut grass.

It is an old story that begins
with a boy whose father's mad and
who stands outside a window listening to
the music inside. And there are grace notes
to this scene; a thrush hidden in a branch
sings relentlessly, until the boy's gaze
repeats itself in the darkened glass.

Years later, limbs circle in the wind
as mosquitoes bite like ideas in the dark
of a porch arranged by rocking chairs.
Two figures talk beyond a lighted door,
tilting over the rigid past
in chairs that arc outside of light,
movement sweeping across wide fields
and dialogue that wills the years revoked.
Here, history is a common fault
revised out of uncommon talk.
Your parents live along a gap that,
waiting there, they cannot see yet argue for.

Watered by another generation,
the fairway's sown promise greens,
though clipped too close to repeat itself.
Overhead, a low cloud's close approach,
racing, is followed by cloud after cloud,
all racing, but to where?
And the general rain dispersing itself,
but toward what end?
One cell divides. Another dies.
The rhythm holds relentlessly.
Is it the ritual or narrative
of our lives we understand?

Towards a Relative Ending

Uninterrupted days occasion us,
affording light, withdrawing light,
almost as if someone too far away
had thought but then forgotten why he thought
or, intuitive, had acted without cause
and, looking again, wondered what it was he meant.

Self-thinking and forgetful at one time,
we live in rooms we know too well
until that ocular day,
vivid for the sky's emptiness:
the desk no more a desk,
bookshelves only a sequence after myth,
each object odd, beyond the schemes
of numbered space and alphabet;

or else a room kept closed too long,
a safe appointed place
imagined as the portal to some end
with light obscured by canopies of dust,
an iridescent dust in winter light
that suddenly draws dark along the floor,
clouds passing miles overhead.

Our Tree of Opposites

I watch you where the wren will wake
Restless and alert, your laughter rising
Above the ash and evergreen,
The wren's insistent music rising
And branches sculling, oars against wind,
A changing current, leaves lifting with
A gust that never circles back.

The weather turns. The season turns,
March into April, limbs fingering leaves
That silhouette reticulate shade
Across the raveled undergrowth;
A reed thrumming in the wind
And the bird, head tilted, watching you,
Your voice cutting inside a shadow's edge.

Most days our tree of opposites
Thickens with a reasoned fruit,
Our discourse balancing solecisms
Under the limb-divided sky.
The wren sings. You stand apart.
I follow a path that runs interior;
The animal I find stands reflexively.

At night, we wait to brave a sleep
That interlocks all the day divides.
Outside, the ash and evergreen are tilting:
In the woods an animal dies,
And seeds take root in the decay until
A tree towers. When light unfolds that tree
The wren will wake and each of us will sing.

Wyatt Prunty has contributed poems and articles to more than thirty periodicals, including the *Southern Review,* the *Virginia Quarterly Review, Salmagundi,* the *New Republic,* the *Georgia Review,* the *Sewanee Review, Canto,* and the *Michigan Quarterly Review.* His chapbook, *Domestic of the Outer Banks,* was published in 1980. *The Times Between* is his first full-length collection of poems.

The Johns Hopkins University Press
This book was composed in Aldine Roman text
type by Horne Associates, Inc., and in Deepdene
Italic and Delphian Open display type by Alpha
Graphics, from a design by Lisa S. Mirski. It was
printed and bound by The Maple Press Co.